HOME

HOME

DAVID STOREY

JONATHAN CAPE
THIRTY BEDFORD SQUARE
LONDON

FIRST PUBLISHED 1970
© 1970 BY DAVID STOREY

JONATHAN CAPE LTD
30 BEDFORD SQUARE, LONDON WC1

ISBN 0 224 00515 4

PRINTED IN GREAT BRITAIN
BY EBENEZER BAYLIS AND SON LTD
THE TRINITY PRESS, WORCESTER, AND LONDON
BOUND BY G. AND J. KITCAT LTD, LONDON

TO KAREL REISZ

WHO FIRST BROUGHT THESE
ENDS TOGETHER

This play was first presented at the Royal Court Theatre, London, on June 17th, 1970, under the direction of Lindsay Anderson. The cast was as follows:

Harry	JOHN GIELGUD
Jack	RALPH RICHARDSON
Marjorie	DANDY NICHOLS
Kathleen	MONA WASHINGTON
Alfred	WARREN CLARKE

CHARACTERS

HARRY
JACK
MARJORIE
KATHLEEN
ALFRED

ACT ONE

Scene 1

The stage is bare but for a round metalwork table, set slightly off-centre, stage left, and two metalwork chairs. *

HARRY comes on, stage right, a middle-aged man in his forties. He wears a casual suit, perhaps tweed, with a suitable hat which, after glancing pleasurably around, he takes off and puts on the table beside him, along with a pair of well-used leather gloves and a folded newspaper.

Presses his shoulders back, eases neck, etc., making himself comfortable. Settles down. Glances at his watch, shakes it, makes sure it's going: winds it slowly, looking round.

Stretches neck again. Leans down, wafts cotton from his turn-ups. Examines shoes, without stooping.

Clears his throat. Clasps his hands in his lap, gazes out, abstracted, head nodding slightly, half-smiling.

JACK. Harry!

> (*JACK has come on from the other side, stage left. He's dressed in a similar fashion, but with a slightly more dandyish flavour: handkerchief hanging from top pocket, a rakish trilby. Also has a simple though rather elegant cane.*)

HARRY. Jack.

JACK. Been here long?

HARRY. No. No.

JACK. Mind?

HARRY. Not at all.

> (*JACK sits down.*
> *He stretches, shows great relief at being off his feet, etc.*)

* In the Royal Court production the indications of a setting were provided: a white flag-pole, stage right, and upstage a low terrace with a single step down, centre, and balustrade, stage left.

9

JACK. Nice to see the sun again.

HARRY. Very.

JACK. Been laid up for a few days.

HARRY. Oh dear.

JACK. Chill. In bed.

HARRY. Oh dear. Still ... Appreciate the comforts.

JACK. What? ... You're right. Still ... Nice to be out.

HARRY. 'Tis.

JACK. Mind?

HARRY. All yours.

(JACK *picks up the paper; gazes at it without unfolding it.*)

JACK. Damn bad news.

HARRY. Yes.

JACK. Not surprising.

HARRY. Gets worse before it gets better.

JACK. 'S right ... Still ... Not to grumble.

HARRY. No. No.

JACK. Put on a bold front. (*Turns paper over.*)

HARRY. That's right.

JACK. Pretty. (*Indicates paper.*)

HARRY. Very.

JACK. By jove ... (*Reads intently a moment.*) Oh, well.

HARRY. That the one? (*Glances over.*)

JACK (*nods*). Yes ... (*Clicks his tongue.*)

HARRY (*shakes his head*). Ah, well.

JACK. Yes ... Still ...

HARRY. Clouds ... Watch their different shapes.

JACK. Yes? (*Looks up at the sky at which* HARRY *is gazing.*)

HARRY. See how they drift over?

JACK. By jove.

HARRY. First sight ... nothing. Then ... just watch the edges ...
See.

JACK. Amazing.

HARRY. Never notice when you're just walking.

JACK. No ... Still ... Best time of the year.

HARRY. What?

JACK. Always think this is the best time.

HARRY. Oh, yes.

JACK. Not too hot. Not too cold.

HARRY. Seen that? (*Points at the paper.*)

JACK (*reads. Then:*) By jove ... (*Reads again briefly.*) Well ... you get some surprises ... Hello ... (*Reads farther down, turning edge of paper over.*) Good God.

HARRY. What I felt.

JACK. The human mind. (*Shakes his head.*)

HARRY. Oh dear, yes.

JACK. One of these days ...

HARRY. Ah, yes.

JACK. Then where will they be?

HARRY. Oh, yes.

JACK. Never give it a thought.

HARRY. No ... Never.

JACK (*reads again*). By jove ... (*Shakes his head.*)

    (HARRY *leans over; removes something casually from* JACK's *sleeve.*)

  Oh ...

HARRY. Cotton.

JACK. Oh ... Picked it up ... (*Glances round at his other sleeve, then down at his trousers.*)

HARRY. See you've come prepared.

JACK. What ... ? Oh.

    (HARRY *indicates* JACK's *coat pocket.*

    JACK *takes out a folded plastic mac, no larger, folded, than his hand.*)

  Best to make sure.

HARRY. Took a risk. Myself.

JACK. Oh, yes ... What's life worth ...

HARRY. Oh, yes.

JACK. I say. That was a shock.

HARRY. Yesterday … ?

JACK. Bolt from the blue, and no mistake.

HARRY. I'd been half-prepared … even then.

JACK. Still a shock.

HARRY. Absolutely.

JACK. My wife … you've met? … Was that last week?

HARRY. Ah, yes …

JACK. Well. A very delicate woman.

HARRY. Still. Very sturdy.

JACK. Oh, well. Physically, nothing to complain of.

HARRY. Oh, no.

JACK. Temperament, however … inclined to the sensitive side.

HARRY. Really.

JACK. Two years ago … (*Glances off.*) By jove. Isn't that Saxton?

HARRY. Believe it is.

JACK. He's a sharp dresser, and no mistake.

HARRY. Very.

JACK. They tell me … Well, I never.

HARRY. Didn't see that, did he?

(*They laugh, looking off.*)

Eyes in the back of your head these days.

JACK. You have. That's right.

HARRY. Won't do that again in a hurry. What? (*Laughs.*)

JACK. I had an uncle once who bred horses.

HARRY. Really.

JACK. Used to go down there when I was a boy.

HARRY. The country.

JACK. Nothing like it. What? Fresh air.

HARRY. Clouds. (*Gestures up.*)

JACK. I'd say so.

HARRY. *My* wife was coming up this morning.

JACK. Really?

HARRY. Slight headache. Thought might be better …

12

JACK. Indoors. Well. Best make sure.

HARRY. When I was in the army ...

JACK. Really? What regiment?

HARRY. Fusiliers.

JACK. Really? How extraordinary.

HARRY. You?

JACK. No. No. A cousin.

HARRY. Well ...

JACK. Different time, of course.

HARRY. Ah.

JACK. Used to bring his rifle ... No. That was Arthur. Got them muddled. (*Laughs.*)

HARRY. Still.

JACK. Never leaves you.

HARRY. No. No.

JACK. In good stead.

HARRY. Oh, yes.

JACK. All your life.

HARRY. Oh, yes.

JACK. I was – for a very short while – in the Royal Air Force.

HARRY. Really?

JACK. Nothing to boast about.

HARRY. Oh, now. Flying?

JACK. On the ground.

HARRY. Chrysanthemums is my wife's hobby.

JACK. Really.

HARRY. Thirty-seven species round the house.

JACK. Beautiful flower.

HARRY. Do you know there are over a hundred?

JACK. Really?

HARRY. Different species.

JACK. Suppose you can mix them up.

HARRY. Oh. Very.

JACK. He's coming back ...

HARRY. ... ?

JACK. Swanson.

HARRY. Saxton.

JACK. Saxton! Always did get those two mixed up. Two boys at school: one called Saxton, the other Swanson. Curious thing was, they both looked alike.

HARRY. Really?

JACK. Both had a curious skin disease. Here. Just at the side of the nose.

HARRY. Eczema.

JACK. Really?

HARRY. Could have been.

JACK. Never thought of that ... When I was young I had an ambition to be a priest, you know.

HARRY. Really?

JACK. Thought about it a great deal.

HARRY. Ah, yes. A great decision.

JACK. Oh, yes.

HARRY. Catholic or Anglican?

JACK. Well ... Couldn't really make up my mind.

HARRY. Both got a great deal to offer.

JACK. Great deal? My word.

HARRY. Advantages one way. And then ... in another.

JACK. Oh, yes.

HARRY. One of my first ambitions ...

JACK. Yes.

HARRY. Oh, now. You'll laugh.

JACK. No. No ... No. Really.

HARRY. Well ... I would have liked to have been a dancer.

JACK. Dancer ... Tap or 'balley'?

HARRY. Oh, well. Probably a bit of both.

JACK. A fine thing. Grace.

HARRY. Ah, yes.

JACK. Physical momentum.

HARRY. Yes.

JACK. Swanson might have appreciated that! (*Laughs.*)

HARRY. Saxton.

JACK. Saxton! By jove ... At school we had a boy called Ramsbottom.

HARRY. Really.

JACK. Now I wouldn't have envied that boy's life.

HARRY. No.

JACK. The euphemisms to which a name ... well. One doesn't have to think very far.

HARRY. No.

JACK. A name can be a great embarrassment in life.

HARRY. It can ... We had—let me think—a boy called Fish.

JACK. Fish!

HARRY. And another called Parsons!

JACK. Parsons!

HARRY. Nicknamed 'Nosey'.

JACK. By jove! (*Laughs; rises.*) Some of these nicknames are very clever.

HARRY. Yes.

JACK (*moves away stage right*). I remember, when I was young, I had a very tall friend ... extremely tall as a matter of fact. He was called 'Lolly'.

HARRY. Lolly!

JACK. It fitted him very well. He ... (*Abstracted. Pause.*) Yes. Had very large teeth as well.

HARRY. The past. It conjures up some images.

JACK. It does. You're right.

HARRY. You wonder how there was ever time for it all.

JACK. Time ... Oh ... Don't mention it.

HARRY. A fine cane.

JACK. What? Oh, that.

HARRY. Father had a cane. Walked for miles.

JACK. A habit that's fast dying out.

HARRY. Oh, yes.

JACK. Knew a man, related to a friend of mine, who used to walk twenty miles a day.

HARRY. Twenty!

JACK. Each morning.

HARRY. That really shows some spirit.

JACK. If you keep up a steady pace, you can manage four miles in the hour.

HARRY. Goodness.

JACK. Five hours. Set off at eight each morning. Back for lunch at one.

HARRY. Must have had a great appetite.

JACK. Oh. Absolutely. Ate like a horse.

HARRY. Stand him in good stead later on.

JACK. Ah, yes ... Killed, you know. In the war.

HARRY. Oh dear.

JACK. Funny thing to work out.

HARRY. Oh, yes.

> (*Pause*)

JACK (*sits*). You do any fighting?

HARRY. What?

JACK. Army.

HARRY. Oh, well, then ... modest amount.

JACK. Nasty business.

HARRY. Oh! Doesn't bear thinking about.

JACK. Two relatives of mine killed in the war.

HARRY. Oh dear.

JACK. You have to give thanks, I must say.

HARRY. Oh, yes.

JACK. Mother's father ... a military man.

HARRY. Yes.

JACK. All his life.

HARRY. He must have seen some sights.

JACK. Oh, yes.

HARRY. Must have all had meaning then.

JACK. Oh, yes. India. Africa. He's buried as a matter of fact in Hong Kong.

HARRY. Really?

JACK. So they tell me. Never been there myself.

HARRY. No.

JACK. Hot climates, I think, can be the very devil if you haven't the temperament.

HARRY. Huh! You don't have to tell me.

JACK. Been there?

HARRY. No, no. Just what one reads.

JACK. Dysentery.

HARRY. Beriberi.

JACK. Yellow fever.

HARRY. Oh dear.

JACK. As well, of course, as all the other contingencies.

HARRY. Oh, yes.

JACK. At times one's glad simply to live on an island.

HARRY. Yes.

JACK. Strange that.

HARRY. Yes.

JACK. Without the sea—all around—civilization would never have been the same.

HARRY. Oh, no.

JACK. The ideals of life, liberty, freedom, could never have been the same—democracy—well, if we'd been living on the Continent, for example.

HARRY. Absolutely.

JACK. Those your gloves?

HARRY. Yes.

JACK. Got a pair like that at home.

HARRY. Yes?

JACK. Very nearly. The seam goes the other way, I think. (*Picks one up to look.*) Yes. It does.

HARRY. A present.

JACK. Really?

HARRY. My wife. At Christmas.

JACK. Season of good cheer.

HARRY. Less and less, of course, these days.

JACK. Oh, my dear man. The whole thing has been ruined. The moment money intrudes ... all feeling goes straight out of the window.

HARRY. Oh, yes.

JACK. I had an aunt once who owned a little shop.

HARRY. Yes?

JACK. Made almost her entire income during the few weeks before Christmas.

HARRY. Really.

JACK. Never seemed to occur to her that there might be some ethical consideration.

HARRY. Oh dear.

JACK. Ah, well.

HARRY. Still ...

JACK. Apart from that, she was a very wonderful person.

HARRY. It's very hard to judge.

JACK. It is.

HARRY. I have a car, for instance.

JACK. Yes?

HARRY. One day, in December, I happened to knock a pedestrian over in the street.

JACK. Oh dear.

HARRY. It was extremely crowded.

JACK. You don't have to tell me. I've seen them.

HARRY. Happened to see something they wanted the other side. Dashed across. Before you know where you are ...

JACK. Not serious, I hope?

HARRY. No. No. No. Fractured arm.

JACK. From that, you know, they might learn a certain lesson.

HARRY. Oh, yes.

JACK. Experience is a stern master.

HARRY. Ah, yes. But then ...

JACK. Perhaps the only one.

HARRY. It is.

JACK. I had a cousin, on my mother's side, who once fell off a cliff.

HARRY. Really.

JACK. Quite a considerable height.

HARRY. Ah, yes.

JACK. Fell into the sea, fortunately. Dazed. Apart from that, quite quickly recovered.

HARRY. Very fortunate.

JACK. Did it for a dare. Only twelve years old at the time.

HARRY. I remember I fell off a cliff, one time.

JACK. Oh dear.

HARRY. Not very high. And there was someone there to catch me. (*Laughs.*)

JACK. They can be very exciting places.

HARRY. Oh, very.

JACK. I remember I once owned a little boat.

HARRY. Really.

JACK. For fishing. Nothing very grand.

HARRY. A fishing man.

JACK. Not really. More an occasional pursuit.

HARRY. I've always been curious about that.

JACK. Yes?

HARRY. 'A solitary figure crouched upon a bank.'

JACK. Never stirring.

HARRY. No. No.

JACK. Can be very tedious, I know.

HARRY. Still. A boat is more interesting.

JACK. Oh, yes. A sort of tradition, really.

HARRY. In the family.

JACK. No. No. More in the ... island, you know.

HARRY. Ah, yes.

JACK. Drake.

HARRY. Yes!

JACK. Nelson.

HARRY. Beatty.

JACK. Sir Walter Raleigh.

HARRY. There was a very fine man ... poet.

JACK. Lost his head, you know.

HARRY. It's surprising the amount of dust that collects in so short a space of time. (*Runs hand lightly over table.*)

JACK. It is. (*Looks round.*) Spot like this, perhaps, attracts it.

HARRY. Yes ... (*Pause*) You never became a priest, then?

JACK. No ... No.

HARRY. Splendid to have a vocation.

JACK. 'Tis ... Something you believe in.

HARRY. Oh, yes.

JACK. I could never ... resolve certain difficulties, myself.

HARRY. Yes?

JACK. The hows and the wherefores I could understand. How we came to be, and His presence, lurking everywhere, you know. But as to the 'why' ... I could never understand. Seemed a terrible waste of time to me.

HARRY. Oh, yes.

JACK. Thought it better to leave it to those who didn't mind.

HARRY. Ah, yes.

JACK. I suppose the same was true about dancing.

HARRY. Oh, yes. I remember turning up for instance, to my first class, only to discover that all the rest of them were girls.

JACK. Really?

HARRY. Well ... there are men dancers, I know. Still ... Took up football after that.

JACK. To professional standard, I imagine.

HARRY. Oh, no. Just the odd kick around. Joined a team that played in the park on Sunday mornings.

JACK. The athletic life has many attractions.

HARRY. It has. It has.

(*Pause*)

JACK. How long have you been here, then?

HARRY. Oh, a couple of er.

JACK. Strange—meeting the other day.

HARRY. Yes.

JACK. On the way back, thought to myself, 'What a chance encounter.'

HARRY. Yes.

JACK. So rare, these days, to meet someone to whom one can actually talk.

HARRY. I know what you mean.

JACK. One works. One looks around. One meets people. But very little communication actually takes place.

HARRY. Very.

JACK. None at all in most cases! (*Laughs.*)

HARRY. Oh, absolutely.

JACK. The agonies and frustrations. I can assure you. In the end one gives up in absolute despair.

HARRY. Oh, yes. (*Laughs, rising, looking off.*)

JACK. Isn't that Parker? (*Looking off*)

HARRY. No ... N-no ... Believe his name is Fielding.

JACK. Could have sworn it was Parker.

HARRY. No. Don't think so ... Parker walks with a limp. Very slight.

JACK. That's Marshall.

HARRY. Really. Then I've got Parker mixed up again. (*Laughs.*)

JACK. Did you see the one who came in yesterday?

HARRY. Hendricks.

JACK. Is that his name?

HARRY. I believe that's what I heard.

JACK. He looked a very suspicious character to me. And his wife ...

HARRY. I would have thought his girl-friend.

JACK. Really? Then that makes far more sense ... I mean, I have great faith in the institution of marriage as such.

HARRY. Oh, yes.

JACK. But one thing I've always noticed. When you find a married couple who display their affection in public, then that's an infallible sign that their marriage is breaking up.

HARRY. Really?

JACK. It's a very curious thing. I'm sure there must be some psychological explanation for it.

HARRY. Insecurity.

JACK. Oh, yes.

HARRY. Quite frequently one can judge people entirely by their behaviour.

JACK. You can. I believe you're right.

HARRY. Take my father, for instance.

JACK. Oh, yes.

HARRY. An extraordinary man by any standard. And yet, throughout his life, he could never put out a light.

JACK. Really.

HARRY. Superstition. If he had to turn off a switch, he'd ask someone else to do it.

JACK. How extraordinary.

HARRY. Quite casually. One never noticed. Over the years one got quite used to it, of course. As a man he was extremely polite.

JACK. Ah, yes.

HARRY (*sits*). Mother, now. She was quite the reverse.

JACK. Oh, yes.

HARRY. Great appetite for life.

JACK. Really?

HARRY. Three.

JACK. Three?

HARRY. Children.

JACK. Ah, yes.

HARRY. Youngest.

JACK. You were?

HARRY. Oh, yes.

JACK. One of seven.

HARRY. Seven!

JACK. Large families in those days.

HARRY. Oh, yes.

JACK. Family life.

HARRY. Oh, yes.

JACK. Society, well, without it, wouldn't be what it's like today.

HARRY. Oh, no.

JACK. Still.

HARRY. Ah, yes.

JACK. We have a wonderful example.

HARRY. Oh. My word.

JACK. At times I don't know where some of us would be without it.

HARRY. No. Not at all.

JACK. A friend of mine—actually, more of an acquaintance, really—was introduced to George VI at Waterloo.

HARRY. Waterloo?

JACK. The station.

HARRY. By jove.

JACK. He was an assistant to the station-master at the time, in a lowly capacity, of course. His Majesty was making a week-end trip into the country.

HARRY. Probably to Windsor.

(*Pause*)

JACK. Can you get to Windsor from Waterloo?

HARRY. I'm ... No. I'm not sure.

JACK. Sandringham, of course, is in the country.

HARRY. The other way.

JACK. The other way.

HARRY. Balmoral in the Highlands.

JACK. I had an aunt once who, for a short while, lived near Gloucester.

HARRY. That's a remarkable stretch of the country.

JACK. Vale of Evesham.

HARRY. Vale of Evesham.

JACK. Local legend has it that Adam and Eve originated there.

HARRY. Really?

JACK. Has very wide currency, I believe, in the district. For instance. You may have read that portion in the Bible ...

HARRY. I have.

JACK. The profusion of vegetation, for example, would indicate that it couldn't, for instance, be anywhere in the Middle East.

HARRY. No. No.

JACK. On the other hand, the profusion of animals ... snakes, for example ... would indicate that it might easily be a more tropical environment, as opposed, that is, to one which is merely temperate.

HARRY. Yes ... I see.

JACK. Then again, there is ample evidence to suggest that during the period in question equatorial conditions prevailed in the very region in which we are now sitting.

HARRY. Really? (*Looks around.*)

JACK. Discoveries have been made that would indicate that lions and tigers, elephants, wolves, rhinoceros, and so forth, actually inhabited these parts.

HARRY. My word.

JACK. In those circumstances, it wouldn't be unreasonable to suppose that the Vale of Evesham was such a place itself. The very cradle, as it were, of ...

HARRY. Close to where your aunt lived.

JACK. That's right.

HARRY. Mind if I have a look?

JACK. Not at all.

(HARRY *takes the cane*.)

HARRY. You seldom see canes of this quality these days.

JACK. No. No. That's right.

HARRY. I believe they've gone out of fashion.

JACK. They have.

HARRY. Like beards.

JACK. Beards!

HARRY. My father had a small moustache.

JACK. A moustache I've always thought became a man.

HARRY. Chamberlain.

JACK. Roosevelt.

HARRY. Schweitzer.

JACK. Chaplin.

HARRY. Hitler ...

JACK. Travel, I've always felt, was a great broadener of the mind.

HARRY. My word.

JACK. Travelled a great deal — when I was young.

HARRY. Far?

JACK. Oh. All over.

HARRY. A great thing.

JACK. Sets its mark upon a man.

HARRY. Like the army.

JACK. Like the army. I suppose the fighting you do has very much the same effect.

HARRY. Oh, yes.

JACK. Bayonet?

HARRY. What?

JACK. The er.

HARRY. Oh, bayonet ... ball and flame. The old three, as we used to call them.

JACK. Ah, yes.

HARRY. A great welder of character.

JACK. By jove.

HARRY. The youth of today: might have done some good.

JACK. Oh. My word, yes.

HARRY. In the Royal Air Force, of course ...

JACK. Bombs.

HARRY. Really.

JACK. Cannon.

HARRY. Ah, yes ... Couldn't have got far, in our job, I can tell you, without the Royal Air Force.

JACK. No. No.

HARRY. Britannia rules the waves ... and rules the skies, too. I shouldn't wonder.

JACK. Oh, yes.

HARRY. Nowadays, of course ...

JACK. Rockets.

HARRY. Ah, yes.

JACK. They say ...

HARRY. Yes?

JACK. When the next catastrophe occurs ...

HARRY. Oh, yes.

JACK. That the island itself might very well be flooded.

HARRY. Really.

JACK. Except for the more prominent peaks, of course.

HARRY. Oh, yes.

JACK. While we're sitting here waiting to be buried ...

HARRY. Oh, yes.

JACK (*laughing*). We'll end up being drowned.

HARRY. Extraordinary! (*Laughs.*) No Vale of Evesham then.

JACK. Oh, no.

HARRY. Nor your aunt at Gloucester!

JACK. She died a little while ago, you know.

HARRY. Oh. I am sorry.

JACK. We weren't very attached.

HARRY. Oh, no.

JACK. Still. She was a very remarkable woman.

HARRY. Ah, yes.

JACK. In her own particular way. So few characters around these days. So few interesting people.

HARRY. Oh, yes.

JACK. Uniformity.

HARRY. Mrs Washington. (*Looking off*)

JACK. Really? I've been keeping an eye open for her.

HARRY. Striking woman.

JACK. Her husband was related to a distant cousin of mine, on my father's side.

HARRY. My word.

JACK. I shouldn't be surprised if she recognizes me ... No ...

HARRY. Scarcely glanced. Her mind on other things.

JACK. Oh, yes.

HARRY. Parker. (*Looking off*)

JACK. Oh, yes.

HARRY. You're right. He's not the man with the limp.

JACK. That's Marshall.

HARRY. That's right. Parker is the one who has something the matter with his arm. I knew it was something like that.

JACK. Polio.

HARRY. Yes?

JACK. I had a sister who contracted polio. Younger than me. Died within a matter of hours.

HARRY. Oh. Goodness.

JACK. Only a few months old at the time. Scarcely learnt to speak.

HARRY. What a terrible experience.

JACK. I had another sister die. She was how old? Eleven.

HARRY. Oh dear.

JACK. Large families do have their catastrophes.

27

HARRY. They do.

JACK. I remember a neighbour of ours, when we lived in the country, died one morning by falling down the stairs.

HARRY. Goodness.

JACK. The extraordinary thing was, the following day they were due to move into a bungalow.

HARRY. Goodness. (*Shakes his head.*)

JACK. One of the great things, of course, about my aunt's house.

HARRY. Yes?

JACK. In Gloucester. Was that it had an orchard.

HARRY. Now they *are* lovely things.

JACK. Particularly in the spring.

HARRY. In the spring especially.

JACK. And the autumn, of course.

HARRY. 'Boughs laden'.

JACK. Apple a day.

HARRY. Oh, yes.

JACK. I had a niece once who was a vegetarian.

HARRY. Really.

JACK. Ate nut rissoles.

HARRY. I tried once to give up meat.

JACK. Goes back, you know.

HARRY. Oh, yes.

JACK. Proctor. The young woman with him is Mrs Jefferies.

HARRY. Really.

JACK. Interesting people to talk to. He's been a missionary, you know.

HARRY. Yes?

JACK. Spent most of his time, he said, taking out people's teeth.

HARRY. Goodness.

JACK. Trained for it, of course. Mrs Jefferies, on the other hand.

HARRY. Yes.

JACK. Was a lady gymnast. Apparently very famous in her day.

HARRY. My word.

JACK. Developed arthritis in two of her er.

HARRY. Oh dear.

JACK. Did you know it was caused by a virus?

HARRY. No.

JACK. Apparently. I had a maiden aunt who suffered from it a great deal. She was a flautist. Played in an orchestra of some distinction. Never married. I thought that very strange.

HARRY. Yes.

JACK. Musicians, of course, are a strange breed altogether.

HARRY. Oh, yes.

JACK. Have you noticed how the best of them have very curly hair?

HARRY. Really.

JACK. My maiden aunt, of course, has died now.

HARRY. Ah, yes.

JACK. Spot of cloud there.

HARRY. Soon passes.

JACK. Ever seen this? (*Takes out a coin.*) There. Nothing up my sleeve. Ready? One, two, three ... Gone.

HARRY. My word.

JACK. Here ... (*Takes out three cards.*) Pick out the Queen of Hearts.

HARRY. This one.

JACK. That's right ... Now ... Queen of Hearts.

HARRY. This one.

JACK. No!

HARRY. Oh!
    (*They laugh.*)

JACK. Try again ... There she is. (*Shuffles them round on the table.*) Where is she?

HARRY. Er ...

JACK. Take your time.

HARRY. This one ... Oh!
    (*They laugh.*)

29

JACK. That one!

HARRY. Well. I'll have to study those.

JACK. Easy when you know how. I have some more back there. One of my favourite tricks is to take the Ace of Spades out of someone's top pocket.

HARRY. Oh ... (*Looks.*)

JACK. No. No. No. (*Laughs.*) It needs some preparation ... Sometimes in a lady's handbag. That goes down very well.

HARRY. Goodness.

JACK. I knew a man at one time—a friend of the family, on my father's side—who could put a lighted cigarette into his mouth, take one half from one ear, and the other half from the other.

HARRY. Goodness.

JACK. Still lighted.

HARRY. How did he do that?

JACK. I don't know.

HARRY. I suppose—physiologically—it's possible, then.

JACK. Shouldn't think so.

HARRY. No.

JACK. One of the advantages, of course, of sitting here.

HARRY. Oh, yes.

JACK. You can see everyone walking past.

HARRY. Oh, yes.

JACK. Jennings isn't a man I'm awfully fond of.

HARRY. No.

JACK. You've probably noticed yourself.

HARRY. I have. In the army, I met a man ... Private ... er.

JACK. The equivalent rank, of course, in the air force, is air-craftsman.

HARRY. Or able seaman. In the navy.

JACK. Able seaman.

　　(*They laugh.*)

HARRY. Goodness.

JACK. Funny name. (*Laughs.*) Able seaman. I don't think I'd like to be called that.

HARRY. Yes! (*Laughs.*)

JACK. Able seaman! (*Snorts.*)

HARRY. Fraser. Have you noticed him?

JACK. Don't think I have.

HARRY. A thin moustache.

JACK. Black.

HARRY. That's right.

JACK. My word.

HARRY. Steer clear, probably, might be better.

JACK. Some people you can sum up at a glance.

HARRY. Oh, yes.

JACK. My mother was like that. Delicate. Not unlike my wife.

HARRY. Nevertheless, very sturdy.

JACK. Oh, yes. Physically, nothing to complain about. My mother, on the other hand, was actually as delicate as she looked. Whereas my wife looks ...

HARRY. Robust.

JACK. Robust. My mother actually looked extremely delicate.

HARRY. Still. Seven children.

JACK. Oh, yes.

HARRY. My father was a very ... emotional man. Of great feeling.

JACK. Like mine.

HARRY. Oh, very much like yours.

JACK. But dominated somewhat.

HARRY. Yes?

JACK. By your mother.

HARRY. Oh. I suppose he was. Passionate but ...

JACK. Dominated. One of the great things, of course, about the war was its feeling of camaraderie.

HARRY. Friendship.

31

JACK. You found that too? On the airfield where I was stationed it was really like one great big happy family. My word. The things one did for one another.

HARRY. Oh, yes.

JACK. The way one worked.

HARRY. Soon passed.

JACK. Oh, yes. It did. It did.

HARRY. Ah, yes.

JACK. No sooner was the fighting over than back it came. Back-biting. Complaints. Getting what you can. I sometimes think if the war had been prolonged another thirty years we'd have all felt the benefit.

HARRY. Oh, yes.

JACK. One's children would have grown up far different. That's for sure.

HARRY. Really? How many have you got?

JACK. Two.

HARRY. Oh, that's very nice.

JACK. Boy married. Girl likewise. They seem to rush into things so early these days.

HARRY. Oh, yes.

JACK. And you?

HARRY. Oh. No. No. Never had the privilege.

JACK. Ah, yes. Responsibility. At times you wonder if it's worth it. I had a cousin, on my father's side, who threw herself from a railway carriage.

HARRY. Oh dear. How awful.

JACK. Yes.

HARRY. Killed outright.

JACK. Well, fortunately, it had just pulled into a station.

HARRY. I see.

JACK. Daughter's married to a salesman. Refrigerators: he sells appliances of that nature.

HARRY. Oh. Opposite to me.

32

JACK. Yes?

HARRY. Heating engineer.

JACK. Really. I'd never have guessed. How extraordinary.

HARRY. And yourself.

JACK. Oh, I've tinkered with one or two things.

HARRY. Ah, yes.

JACK. What I like about my present job is the scope that it leaves you for initiative.

HARRY. Rather. Same with mine.

JACK. Distribution of food-stuffs in a wholesale store.

HARRY. Really.

JACK. Thinking out new ideas. Constant speculation.

HARRY. Oh, yes.

JACK. Did you know if you put jam into small cardboard containers it will sell far better than if you put it into large glass jars?

HARRY. Really?

JACK. Psychological. When you buy it in a jar you're wondering what on earth — subconsciously — you're going to do with the glass bottle. But with a cardboard box that anxiety is instantly removed. Result: improved sales: improved production; lower prices; improved distribution.

HARRY. That's a fascinating job.

JACK. Oh, yes. If you use your brains there's absolutely nothing there to stop you.

HARRY. I can see.

JACK. Heating must be a very similar problem.

HARRY. Oh, yes.

JACK. The different ways of warming up a house.

HARRY. Yes.

JACK. Or not warming it up, as the case may be.

HARRY. Yes!

(*They laugh.*)

JACK. I don't think I've met your wife.

C
33

HARRY. No. No ... As a matter of fact. We've been separated
for a little while.

JACK. Oh dear.

HARRY. One of those misfortunes.

JACK. Happens a great deal.

HARRY. Oh, yes.

JACK. Each have our cross.

HARRY. Oh, yes.

JACK. Well. Soon be time for lunch.

HARRY. Will. And I haven't had my walk.

JACK. No. Still.

HARRY. Probably do as much good.

JACK. Oh, yes.

HARRY. Well, then ... (*Stretches. Gets up.*)

JACK. Yours or mine?

HARRY. Mine ... I believe. (*Picks up the newspaper.*)

JACK. Ah, yes.

HARRY. Very fine gloves.

JACK. Yes.

HARRY. Pacamac.

JACK. All correct.

HARRY. Cane.

JACK. Cane.

HARRY. Well, then. Off we go.

JACK. Off we go.

    (HARRY *breathes in deeply; breathes out.*)

HARRY. Beautiful corner.

JACK. 'Tis.

    (*Pause; last look round.*)

HARRY. Work up an appetite.

JACK. Right, then. Best foot forward.

HARRY. Best foot forward.

JACK. Best foot forward, and off we go.

    (*They stroll off, taking the air, stage left.*)

34

Scene 2

KATHLEEN *and* MARJORIE *come on, stage right.*

KATHLEEN *is a stout middle-aged lady; she wears a coat, which is unbuttoned, a headscarf, and strap shoes. She is limping, her arm supported by* MARJORIE.

MARJORIE *is also middle-aged. She is dressed in a skirt and cardigan. She carries an umbrella and a large, well-used bag.*

KATHLEEN. Cor ... *blimey!*

MARJORIE. Going to rain, ask me.

KATHLEEN. Rain all it wants, ask me. Cor ... *blimey!* Going to kill me is this. (*Limps to a chair, sits down and holds her foot.*)

MARJORIE. Going to rain and catch us out here. That's what it's going to do. (*Puts umbrella up: worn, but not excessively so.*)

KATHLEEN. Going to rain all right, i'n't it? Going to rain all right ... Put your umbrella up—sun's still shining. Cor blimey. Invite rain that will. Commonsense, girl ... Cor *blimey* ... My bleedin' feet ... (*Rubs one foot without removing shoe.*)

MARJORIE. Out here and no shelter. Be all right if it starts. (*Moves umbrella one way then another, looking up.*)

KATHLEEN. Cor *blimey* ... 'Surprise me they don't drop off ... Cut clean through, these will.

MARJORIE (*looking skywards, however*). Clouds all over. Told you we shouldn't have come out.

KATHLEEN. Get nothing if you don't try, girl ... Cor *blimey!* (*Winces.*)

MARJORIE. I don't know.

KATHLEEN. Here. You'll be all right, won't you?

MARJORIE. ... ?

KATHLEEN. Holes there is. See right through, you can.

MARJORIE. What?

KATHLEEN. Here. Rain come straight through that. Won't get much shelter under that. What d'I tell you? Might as well sit under a shower. (*Laughs.*) Cor blimey. You'll be all right, won't you?

MARJORIE. Be all right with you in any case. Walk no faster than a snail.

KATHLEEN. Not surprised. Don't want me to escape. That's my trouble, girl.

MARJORIE. Here ...

> (JACK *and* HARRY *slowly pass upstage, taking the air, chatting.*
>
> MARJORIE *and* KATHLEEN *wait for them to pass.*)

KATHLEEN. What've we got for lunch?

MARJORIE. Sprouts.

KATHLEEN (*massaging foot*). Seen them, have you?

MARJORIE. Smelled 'em!

KATHLEEN. What's today, then?

MARJORIE. Friday.

KATHLEEN. End of week.

MARJORIE. Corn' beef hash.

KATHLEEN. That's Wednesday.

MARJORIE. Sausage roll.

KATHLEEN. Think you're right ... Cor *blimey.* (*Groans, holding her foot.*)

MARJORIE. Know what you ought to do, don't you?

> (KATHLEEN *groans holding her foot.*)

Ask for another pair of shoes, girl, you ask me.

KATHLEEN. Took me laced ones, haven't they? Only ones that fitted. Thought I'd hang myself, didn't they? Only five inches long.

MARJORIE. What they think you are?

KATHLEEN. Bleedin' mouse, more likely.

MARJORIE. Here. Not like the last one I was in.

KATHLEEN. No?

MARJORIE. Let you paint on the walls, they did. Do anyfing.
Just muck around ... Here ... I won't tell you what some of
them did.

KATHLEEN. What?

(MARJORIE *leans over, whispers.*)
Never.

MARJORIE. Cross me heart.

KATHLEEN. Glad I wasn't there. This place is bad enough. You
seen Henderson, have you?

MARJORIE. Ought to lock him up, you ask me.

KATHLEEN. What d'you do, then?

MARJORIE. Here?

KATHLEEN. At this other place.

MARJORIE. Noffing. Mucked around ...

KATHLEEN. Here ...

(JACK *and* HARRY *stroll back again, slowly, upstage, in
conversation; head back, deep breathing, bracing arms ...*
MARJORIE *and* KATHLEEN *wait till they pass.*)

MARJORIE. My dentist comes from Pakistan.

KATHLEEN. Yours?

MARJORIE. Took out all me teeth.

KATHLEEN. Those not your own, then?

MARJORIE. All went rotten when I had my little girl. There she
is, waitress at the seaside.

KATHLEEN. And you stuck here ...

MARJORIE. No teeth ...

KATHLEEN. Don't appreciate it.

MARJORIE. They don't.

KATHLEEN. Never.

MARJORIE. Might take this down if it doesn't rain.

KATHLEEN. Cor blimey ... take these off if I thought I could
get 'em on again ... (*Groans.*) Tried catching a serious
disease.

MARJORIE. When was that?

KATHLEEN. Only had me in two days. Said, nothing the matter with you, my girl.

MARJORIE. Don't believe you.

KATHLEEN. Next thing: got home; smashed everything in sight.

MARJORIE. No?

KATHLEEN. Winders. Cooker ... Nearly broke me back ... Thought I'd save the telly. Still owed eighteen months. Thought: 'Everything or nothing, girl.'

MARJORIE. Rotten programmes.

KATHLEEN. Didn't half give it a good old conk.

MARJORIE (*looking round*). There's one thing. You get a good night's sleep.

KATHLEEN. Like being with a steam engine, where I come from. Cor blimey, that much whistling and groaning; think you're going to take off.

MARJORIE More like a boa constrictor, ask me. Here ...

(JACK *and* HARRY *stroll back, still taking the air, upstage; bracing, head back ...*)

Started crying everywhere I went ... Started off on Christmas Eve.

KATHLEEN. 'S'happy time, Christmas.

MARJORIE. Didn't stop till Boxing Day.

KATHLEEN. If He ever comes again I hope He comes on Whit Tuesday. For me that's the best time of the year.

MARJORIE. Why's that?

KATHLEEN. Dunno. Whit Tuesday's always been a lucky day for me. First party I ever went to was on a Whit Tuesday. First feller I went with. Can't be the date. Different every year.

MARJORIE. My lucky day's the last Friday in any month with an 'r' in it when the next month doesn't begin later than the following Monday.

KATHLEEN. How do you make that out?

MARJORIE. Dunno. I was telling the doctor that the other day ... There's that man with the binoculars watching you.

KATHLEEN. Where?

MARJORIE. Lift your dress up.

KATHLEEN. No.

MARJORIE. Go on … (*Leans over; does it for her.*) Told you …

KATHLEEN. Looks like he's got diarrhoea!
   (*They laugh.*)
   See that chap the other day? Showed his slides of a trip up the Amazon River.

MARJORIE. See that one with no clothes on? Supposed to be cooking his dinner.

KATHLEEN. Won't have him here again …

MARJORIE. Showing all his ps and qs.

KATHLEEN. Ooooooh! (*Laughs, covering her mouth.*)

MARJORIE. Here …
   (JACK *and* HARRY *stroll back across, a little farther downstage, glancing over now at* MARJORIE *and* KATHLEEN.)

KATHLEEN. Lord and Lady used to live here at one time.

MARJORIE. Who's that?

KATHLEEN. Dunno.

MARJORIE. Probably still inside, ask me … (*Glances after* JACK *and* HARRY *as they stroll off.*) See that woman with dyed hair? Told me she'd been in films. 'What films?' I said. 'Blue films?'

KATHLEEN. What she say?

MARJORIE. 'The ones I was in was not in colour.'
   (*They laugh.*)
   I s'll lose me teeth one of these days … oooh!

KATHLEEN. Better'n losing something else …

MARJORIE. Ooooh!
   (*They laugh again.*)

KATHLEEN. Here …
   (JACK *and* HARRY *have strolled back on.*)

JACK (*removing hat*). Good day, ladies.

KATHLEEN. Good day yourself, your lordships.

JACK. Oh, now. I wouldn't go as far as that. (*Laughs politely and looks at* HARRY.)

HARRY. No. No. Still a bit of the common touch.

JACK. Least, so I'd hope.

HARRY. Oh, yes.

MARJORIE. And how have you been keeping, professor?

JACK. Professor? I can see we're a little elevated today.

MARJORIE. Don't know about elevated. But *we*'re sitting down. (KATHLEEN *and* MARJORIE *laugh*.)

KATHLEEN. Been standing up, we have, for hours.

HARRY. Hours?

MARJORIE. When you were sitting down.

JACK. Oh dear … I wasn't aware …

KATHLEEN. 'Course you were. My bleedin' feet. Just look at them. (*Holds them again*.)

MARJORIE. Pull your skirt down, girl.

KATHLEEN. Oh Gawd …

JACK. My friend here, Harry, is a specialist in house-warming, and I myself am a retailer in preserves.

MARJORIE. Oooooh! (*Screeches; laughs—covering her mouth—to* KATHLEEN.) What did I tell you?

KATHLEEN. No atomic bombs today?

JACK (*looks up at the sky behind him. Then:*) No, no. Shouldn't think so.

MARJORIE. And how's your mongol sister?

HARRY. Mongol … ? I'm afraid you must have the wrong person, Ma'm.

KATHLEEN. Ooooh! (*Screeches; laughs*.)

JACK. My friend, I'm afraid, is separated from his wife. As a consequence, I can assure you, of many hardships …

MARJORIE. Of course …

JACK. And I myself, though happily married in some respects, would not pretend that my situation is all it should be …

KATHLEEN. Ooooh!

JACK. One endeavours ... but it is in the nature of things, I believe, that, on the whole, one fails.

KATHLEEN. Ooooh!

HARRY. My friend ... Jack ... has invented several new methods of retailing jam.

KATHLEEN. Ooooh!

MARJORIE. Jam. I like that.

JACK. Really?

MARJORIE (to KATHLEEN). Strawberry. My favourite.

KATHLEEN. Raspberry, mine.

MARJORIE. Ooooh!

(KATHLEEN and MARJORIE laugh.)

JACK. A friend of mine, on my father's side, once owned a small factory which was given over, exclusively, to its manufacture.

KATHLEEN. Ooooh!

JACK. In very large vats.

KATHLEEN. Ooooh!

MARJORIE. I like treacle myself.

JACK. Treacle, now, is a very different matter.

MARJORIE. Comes from Malaya.

HARRY. That's rubber, I believe.

MARJORIE. In tins.

HARRY. The rubber comes from Malaya, I believe.

MARJORIE. I eat it, don't I? I ought to know.

KATHLEEN. She has treacle on her bread.

JACK. I believe it comes, as a matter of fact, from the West Indies.

KATHLEEN. West Indies? Where's that?

MARJORIE. Near Hong Kong.

HARRY. That's the East Indies, I believe.

MARJORIE. You ever been to the North Indies?

HARRY. I don't believe ...

MARJORIE. Well, that's where treacle comes from.

HARRY. I see ...

(Pause. The tone has suddenly become serious.)

JACK. We were just remarking, as a matter of fact, that Mrs Glover isn't looking her usual self.

KATHLEEN. Who's she?

HARRY. She's ...

JACK. The lady with the rather embarrassing disfigurement ...

MARJORIE. Her with one ear?

KATHLEEN. The one who's only half a nose.

MARJORIE. She snores.

KATHLEEN. You'd snore as well, wouldn't you, if you only had half a nose.

MARJORIE. Eaten away.

KATHLEEN. What?

MARJORIE. Her husband ate it one night when she was sleeping.

KATHLEEN. Silly to fall asleep with any man, I say. These days they get up to anything. Read it in the papers an' next thing they want to try it themselves.

HARRY. The weather's been particularly mild today.

KATHLEEN. Not like my flaming feet. Oooh ...

JACK. As one grows older these little things are sent to try us.

KATHLEEN. Little? Cor blimey; I take size seven.

HARRY. My word.

JACK. My friend, of course, in the heating business, has a wide knowledge of the ways and means whereby we may, as we go along, acquire these little additional comforts.

MARJORIE. He wishes he was sitting in this chair, doesn't he?

HARRY. What ...

JACK. It's extraordinary that more facilities of this nature aren't supplied, in my view.

KATHLEEN. Only bit of garden with any flowers. Half a dozen daisies ...

HARRY. Tulips ...

JACK. Roses ...

KATHLEEN. I know daisies, don't I? Those are daisies. Grow three feet tall.

HARRY. Really?

MARJORIE. Rest of it's all covered in muck.

JACK. Oh, now. Not as bad as that.

MARJORIE. What? I call that muck. What's it supposed to be?

HARRY. A rockery, I believe.

KATHLEEN. Rockery? More like a rubbish tip, ask me.

JACK. Probably the flowers haven't grown yet.

MARJORIE. Flowers? How do you grow flowers on old bricks and bits of plaster?

HARRY. Certain categories, of course ...

JACK. Oh, yes.

HARRY. Can be trained to grow in these conditions.

KATHLEEN. You're round the bend, you are. Ought to have you up there, they did.

HARRY (*to* JACK). They tell me the flowers are just as bad at that end, too.

(HARRY *and* JACK *laugh at their private joke.*)

MARJORIE. If you ask me, all this is just typical.

JACK. Typical?

MARJORIE. One table. Two chairs ... Between one thousand people.

KATHLEEN. Two, they tell me.

MARJORIE. Two thousand. One thousand for this chair, and one thousand for that.

HARRY. There are, of course, the various benches.

KATHLEEN. Benches? Seen better sold for firewood.

MARJORIE. Make red marks they do across your bum.

KATHLEEN. Ooooh! (*Screeches, covering her mouth.*)

HARRY. Clouding slightly.

JACK. Slightly. (*Looking up.*)

MARJORIE. Pull your skirt down, girl.

KATHLEEN. Oooh!

HARRY. Of course, one alternative would be to bring, say, a couple of more chairs out with us.

JACK. Oh, yes. Now that would be a solution.

HARRY. Four chairs. One each. I don't believe, say, for an afternoon they'd be missed from the lecture hall.

MARJORIE. Here, you see *Up the Amazon* last night?

JACK. Tuesday ...

HARRY. Tuesday.

JACK. Believe I did, now you mention it.

MARJORIE. See that feller with a loincloth?

KATHLEEN. Ooooh! (*Laughs, covering her mouth.*)

JACK. I must admit, there are certain attractions in the primitive life.

KATHLEEN. Ooooh!

JACK. Air, space ...

MARJORIE. Seen all he's got, that's all you seen.

JACK. I believe there was a moment when the eye ...

KATHLEEN. Moment ... Ooooh!

HARRY. I thought his pancakes looked rather nice.

KATHLEEN. Ooooh!

HARRY. On the little log ...

KATHLEEN. Ooooh!

MARJORIE. Not his pancakes he's seen, my girl.

KATHLEEN. Ooooh!

JACK. The canoe, now, was not unlike my own little boat.

KATHLEEN. Ooooh!

HARRY. Fishing there somewhat more than a mere pastime.

JACK. Oh, yes.

HARRY. Life and death.

JACK. Oh, yes.

MARJORIE. Were you the feller they caught climbing out of a window here last week?

JACK. Me?

MARJORIE. Him.

HARRY. Don't think so ... Don't recollect that.

JACK. Where, if you don't mind me asking, did you acquire that information?

MARJORIE. Where? (*To* KATHLEEN) Here, I thought you told me it was him.

KATHLEEN. Not me. Mrs Heller.

MARJORIE. You sure?

KATHLEEN. Not me, anyway.

JACK. I had a relative-nephew, as a matter of fact — who started a window-cleaning business ... let me see. Three years ago now.

HARRY. Really?

JACK. Great scope there for an adventurous man.

MARJORIE. In bathroom windows 'specially.

KATHLEEN. Ooooh!

JACK. Heights ... distances ...

HARRY. On very tall buildings, of course, they lower them from the roof.

JACK. Oh, yes.

HARRY. Don't have the ladders long enough, you know.

KATHLEEN. Ooooh!

JACK. Your friend seems in a very jovial frame of mind.

HARRY. Like to see that.

JACK. Oh, yes. Gloom: one sees it far too much in this place. Mr Metcalf, now: I don't think he's spoken to anyone since the day that he arrived.

MARJORIE. What's he, then?

HARRY. He's the gentleman who's constantly pacing up and down.

JACK. One says hello, of course. He scarcely seems to notice.

KATHLEEN. Hear you were asking if they'd let you out.

JACK. Who?

MARJORIE. Your friend.

HARRY. Oh. Nothing as dramatic ... Made certain inquiries ... temporary visit ... Domestic problems, you know. Without a man very little, I'm afraid, gets done.

MARJORIE. It gets too much done, if you ask me. That's half the trouble.

KATHLEEN. Oooooh!

HARRY. However ... It seems that certain aspects of it can be cleared up by correspondence. One doesn't wish, after all, to impose unduly ...

JACK. Oh, no.

HARRY. Events have their own momentum. Take their time.

MARJORIE. You married to me, they would. I can tell you.

KATHLEEN. Oooooh!

HARRY. Oh, now ... Missis ... er ...

MARJORIE. Madam.

KATHLEEN. Oooooh!

HARRY. Well ... er ... that might be a situation that could well be beneficial to us both, in different circumstances, in different places ...

JACK. Quite ...

MARJORIE. Listen to him!

HARRY. We all have our little foibles, our little failings.

JACK. Oh, indeed.

HARRY. Hardly be human without.

JACK. Oh, no.

HARRY. The essence of true friendship, in my view, is to make allowances for one another's little lapses.

MARJORIE. Heard all about your little lapses, haven't we?

KATHLEEN. Ooooooh!

JACK. All have our little falls from grace.

MARJORIE. Pull your skirt down, girl!

KATHLEEN. Ooooooh!

MARJORIE. Burn down the whole bleedin' building, he will. Given up smoking because they won't let him have any matches.

KATHLEEN. Oooh!

JACK. The rumours that drift around a place like this ... hardly worth the trouble ...

HARRY. Absolutely.

JACK. If one believed everything one heard ...

HARRY. Oh, yes.

JACK. I was remarking to my friend earlier this morning: if one can't enjoy life as it takes one, what's the point of living it at all? One can't, after all, spend the whole of one's life inside a shell.

HARRY. Oh, no.

MARJORIE. Know what he'd spend it inside if he had half a chance.

KATHLEEN. Ooooooh!

MARJORIE. Tell my husband of you, I shall.

KATHLEEN. Bus-driver.

JACK. Really? I've taken a lifelong interest in public transport.

KATHLEEN. Oooh!

MARJORIE. Taken a lifelong interest in something else more 'n likely.

KATHLEEN. Ooooooh!

MARJORIE. Pull your skirt down, girl!

KATHLEEN. Oooooh!

MARJORIE. Know his kind.

KATHLEEN. Ooooooh!

JACK. Respect for the gentler sex, I must say, is a fast diminishing concept in the modern world.

HARRY. Oh, yes.

JACK. I recollect the time when one stood for a lady as a matter of course.

HARRY. Oh, yes.

MARJORIE. Know the kind of standing he's on about.

KATHLEEN. Ooooooh!

JACK. Each becomes hardened to his ways.

KATHLEEN. Ooooooh!

JACK. No regard for anyone else's.

MARJORIE. Be missing your dinner, you will.

JACK. Yes. So it seems.

HARRY. Late ...

JACK. Nevertheless, one breaks occasionally one's usual ... Normally it's of benefit to all concerned ...

MARJORIE. Here. Are you all right?

JACK. Slight moment of discomposure ...

 (JACK *has begun to cry, vaguely. Takes out a handkerchief to wipe his eyes.*)

HARRY. My friend is a man—he won't mind me saying this ...

JACK. No ... no ...

HARRY. Of great sensibility and feeling.

KATHLEEN. Here. You having us on?

JACK. I assure you, madam ... I regret any anxiety or concern which I may, unwittingly, have caused. In fact—I'm sure my friend will concur—perhaps you'll allow us to accompany you to the dining-hall. I have noticed, in the past, that though one has to queue, to leave it any later is to run the risk of being served with a cold plate; the food cold, and the manners of the cook—at times, I must confess ... appalling.

KATHLEEN (*to* MARJORIE). We'll have to go. There'll be nothing left.

MARJORIE. It's this seat he's after.

HARRY. I assure you, madam ... we are on our way.

KATHLEEN. Here: you mind if I lean on your arm?

MARJORIE. Kathleen!

HARRY. Oh, now. That's a very pretty name.

KATHLEEN. Got straps: make your ankles swell. (*Rising*)

HARRY. Allow me.

KATHLEEN. Oh. Thank you.

HARRY. Harry.

KATHLEEN. Harry.

HARRY. And this is my friend—Jack.

KATHLEEN. Jack ... And this is my friend Marjorie.

JACK. Marjorie ... Delightful.

MARJORIE (*to* KATHLEEN). Here. You all right?

KATHLEEN. You carrying it with you, or are you coming?

JACK. Allow me ... Marjorie. (*Holds her seat.*)

MARJORIE. Here ... (*Gets up, suspicious.*)

HARRY. Perhaps after lunch we might meet here again.

JACK. A little chat ... Time passes very slowly.

MARJORIE. Here, where's my bag?

KATHLEEN. Need carrying out, I will.

 (HARRY *has taken* KATHLEEN's *arm.*)

HARRY. Now then. All right?

KATHLEEN. Have you all the time, I shall.

HARRY. Ready? ... All aboard then, are we?

MARJORIE. Well, then. All right ... (*Takes* JACK's *arm.*)

JACK. Right, then ... Dining-hall: here we come!

 (*They start off,* HARRY *and* KATHLEEN *in front; slowly.*)

HARRY. Sausages today, if I'm not mistaken.

KATHLEEN. Oooh!

MARJORIE. Corned beef hash.

KATHLEEN. Oooh!

JACK. One as good as another, I always say.

KATHLEEN. Oooooh!

HARRY. Turned out better.

JACK. Turned out better.

HARRY. Altogether.

JACK. Altogether.

HARRY. Well, then. Here we go.

 (*They go.*)

ACT TWO

ALFRED *comes in: a well-made young man, about thirty. His jacket's unbuttoned; he has no tie.*

He sees the table; walks past it, slowly, eyeing it. Pauses. Glances back at it.

Comes back, watching the table rather furtively, sideways.

He pauses, hands behind his back, regarding it.

Suddenly he moves towards it, grasps it; struggles with it as if it had a life of its own.

Groans. Struggles. Lifts the table finally above his head.

Struggles with it ...

MARJORIE *comes on, as before, her umbrella furled.*

MARJORIE. Here. You all right?

ALFRED. What?

MARJORIE. Alfred, i'n'it?

ALFRED. Yeh. (*Still holds the table above his head.*)

MARJORIE. You'll break that, you will.

ALFRED. Yeh ... (*Looks up at it.*)

> (MARJORIE, *however, isn't much interested; she's already looking round.*)

MARJORIE. You seen my mate?

ALFRED. ... ?

MARJORIE. Woman that limps.

ALFRED. No.

> (ALFRED *pauses before all his answers.*)

MARJORIE. One day you get seconds and they go off without you. You like treacle pud?

ALFRED. Yeh.

MARJORIE. Get seconds?

ALFRED. No.

MARJORIE. Shoulda waited.

ALFRED. Yeh.

MARJORIE. Said they'd be out here after 'Remedials'.

ALFRED. ... ?

MARJORIE. You do remedials?

ALFRED. Yeh.

MARJORIE. What 'you do?

ALFRED. Baskets.

MARJORIE. Baskets. Shoulda known.

ALFRED. You got sixpence?

MARJORIE. No.

> (ALFRED *lifts the table up and down ceremoniously above his head.*)

Better go find her. Let anybody turn them round her hand, she will.

ALFRED. Yeh.

> (*She goes.*
>
> ALFRED *lowers the table slowly, almost like a ritual.*
>
> *Crouches; picks up one chair by the foot of one leg and lifts it, slowly, exaggerating the effort, etc.*
>
> *Stands, slowly, as he gets it up.*
>
> *Bends arm slowly; lifts the chair above his head.*
>
> *Puts it down.*
>
> *Stands a moment, gazing down at the two chairs and the table, sideways.*
>
> *Walks round them.*
>
> *Walks round a little farther. Then:*
>
> *Grabs the second chair and lifts it, one-handed, like the first chair, but more quickly.*
>
> *Lifts it above his head; begins to wrestle with it as if it too possessed a life of its own, his grip, however, still one-handed.*
>
> MARJORIE *crosses upstage, pauses, looks, walks on.*
>
> *She goes off;* ALFRED *doesn't see her.*
>
> ALFRED *struggles; overcomes the chair.*

Almost absent-mindedly lowers it, looks left, looks right,
casually; puts the chair beneath his arm and goes.)

KATHLEEN (*off*). Oh Gawd ... Oh ... Nah, this side's better ...
Oh.

(*Comes on limping, her arm in* HARRY'*s.*
HARRY *carries a wicker chair under his other arm.*)

HARRY. Oh. Look at that.

KATHLEEN. Where's the other one gone, then?

HARRY. Well, that's a damned nuisance.

KATHLEEN. Still only two. Don't know what they'll say.

HARRY. Oh dear.

KATHLEEN. Pinch anything round here. Can't turn your back.
Gawd ... !

(*Sinks down in the metal chair as* HARRY *holds it for her.*)

HARRY. There, now.

KATHLEEN (*sighs*). Good to get off your feet ...

HARRY. Yes, well ...

(*Sets his own chair to get the sun, fussing.*)

KATHLEEN. Better sit on it. No good standing about. Don't
know where she's got to. Where's your friend looking?

HARRY. Went to 'Remedials', I believe.

KATHLEEN. Get you in there won't let you out again. Here ...

(HARRY *looks across.*)

He really what he says he is?

HARRY. How do you mean?

KATHLEEN. Told us he was a doctor. Another time he said he'd
been a sanitary inspector.

HARRY. Really? Hadn't heard of that.

KATHLEEN. Go on. Know what inspecting he'll do. You the
same.

HARRY. Oh, now. Certain discriminations can be ...

KATHLEEN. I've heard about you.

HARRY. Oh, well, you er.

KATHLEEN. Making up things.

53

HARRY. Oh, well. One ... embodies ... of course.

KATHLEEN. What's that, then?

HARRY. Fancies ... What's life for if you can't ... (*Flutters his fingers.*)

KATHLEEN. We've heard about that an' all. (*Imitates his action.*)

HARRY. Well. I'm sure you and I have, in reality, a great deal in common. After all, one looks around; what does one see?

KATHLEEN. Gawd ... (*Groans, feeling her feet.*)

HARRY. A little this. A little that.

KATHLEEN. Here. Everything you know is little.

HARRY. Well ... I er ... Yes ... No great role for this actor, I'm afraid. A little stage, a tiny part.

KATHLEEN. You an actor, then?

HARRY. Well, I did, as a matter of fact, at one time ... actually, a little ...

KATHLEEN. Here, little again. You notice?

HARRY. Oh ... You're right.

KATHLEEN. What parts you play, then?

HARRY. Well, as a matter of fact ... not your Hamlets, of course, your Ophelias; more the little bystander who passes by the ...

KATHLEEN. Here. Little.

HARRY. Oh ... yes! (*Laughs.*)

KATHLEEN. Play anything romantic?

HARRY. Oh, romance, now, was ... never very far away.

KATHLEEN. Here ...

HARRY. One was cast, of course ...

KATHLEEN. Think I could have been romantic.

HARRY. Oh, yes.

KATHLEEN. Had the chance ... Got it here.

HARRY. Oh, yes ...

KATHLEEN. Had different shoes than this ...

HARRY. Oh, yes ... everything, of course, provided ...

KATHLEEN. Going to be a commotion, you ask me ...

HARRY. Commotion ... ?

KATHLEEN. When they get here.

(*Indicates chairs.*)

Three chairs—if he brings one as well ... He'll have to stand. (*Laughs.*)

HARRY. Could have been confiscated, you know.

KATHLEEN. Confiscated?

HARRY. Often happens. See a little pleasure and down they come.

KATHLEEN. Here ... little.

HARRY. Goodness ... Yes.

(*Pause*)

One of the advantages of this spot, you know, is that it catches the sun so nicely.

KATHLEEN. What bit there is of it.

HARRY. Bit?

KATHLEEN. All that soot. Cuts it down. 'Stead of browning you turns you black.

HARRY. Black?

KATHLEEN. All over.

HARRY. An industrial nation ...

KATHLEEN. Gawd ... (*Eases her feet.*)

HARRY. Can't have the benefit of both. Nature as well as er ... The one is incurred at the expense of the other.

KATHLEEN. Your friend come in for following little girls?

HARRY. What ...

KATHLEEN. Go on. You can tell me. Cross me heart and hope to die.

HARRY. Well ... that's ...

KATHLEEN. Well, then.

HARRY. I believe there were ... er ... certain proclivities, shall we say?

KATHLEEN. Proclivities? What's them?

HARRY. Nothing criminal, of course.

KATHLEEN. Oh, no ...

55

HARRY. No prosecution ...

KATHLEEN. Oh, no ...

HARRY. Certain pressures, in the er ... Revealed themselves.

KATHLEEN. In public?

HARRY. No. No ... I ... Not what I meant.

KATHLEEN. I don't know what you're saying half the time. You realize that?

HARRY. Communication is a difficult factor.

KATHLEEN. Say that again.

HARRY. I believe he was encouraged to come here for a little er.

KATHLEEN. Here. Little.

HARRY. Oh, yes ... As it is, very few places left now where one can be at ease.

KATHLEEN. Could go on his holidays. Seaside.

HARRY. Beaches? ... Crowded all the while.

KATHLEEN. Could go to the country.

HARRY. Spaces ...

KATHLEEN. Sent me to the country once. All them trees. Worse'n people ... Gawd. Take them off if I thought I could get them on again. Can't understand why they don't let me have me laces. Took me belt as well. Who they think I'm going to strangle? Improved my figure, it did, the belt. Drew it in a bit.

HARRY. Oh, now, I would say, myself, the proportions were in reasonable condition.

KATHLEEN. Oh, now ...

HARRY. Without, of course, wishing to seem immodest ...

KATHLEEN. Get little enough encouragement in my life. Gawd ... My friend, you know, was always crying.

HARRY. Oh, now.

KATHLEEN. Everywhere she went ... cigarettes ... No sooner in the shop, opens her mouth, and out it comes. Same on buses.

HARRY. Oh dear, now.

KATHLEEN. Doesn't like sympathy.

HARRY. Ah, yes.

KATHLEEN. Get all I can, myself.

HARRY. Husband a bus-driver, I believe.

KATHLEEN. Hers. Not mine.

HARRY. Ah, yes.

KATHLEEN. Mine's a corporation employee.

HARRY. Ah, yes. One of the ...

KATHLEEN. Cleans up muck. Whenever there's a pile of muck they send him to clean it up.

HARRY. I see.

KATHLEEN. You worked in a bank, then?

HARRY. Well, in a er.

KATHLEEN. Clean job. Don't know why he doesn't get a clean job. Doorman ... Smells awful, he does. Gets bathed one night and the next day just the same.

HARRY. Ah, yes.

KATHLEEN. Puts you off your food.

HARRY. Yes.

KATHLEEN. 'They ought to fumigate you,' I said.

HARRY. Yes?

KATHLEEN. Know what he says?

HARRY. Yes?

KATHLEEN. 'Ought to fumigate you, my girl, and forget to switch it orf.'

HARRY. Goodness.

KATHLEEN. Going to be tea-time before they get here.

HARRY (examines watch). No, no. Still a little time.

KATHLEEN. Your wife alive?

HARRY. Er.

KATHLEEN. Separated?

HARRY. Well, I ...

KATHLEEN. Unsympathetic.

HARRY. Yes?

57

KATHLEEN. Your wife.

HARRY. Well … One can ask too much these days, I believe, of er.

KATHLEEN. Met once a fortnight wouldn't be any divorce. Ridiculous, living together. 'S not human.

HARRY. No …

KATHLEEN. Like animals … Even they run off when they're not feeling like it.

HARRY. Oh, yes.

KATHLEEN. Not natural … One man. One woman. Who's He think He is?

(HARRY *looks round.*)

No … Him. (*Points up*)

HARRY. Oh, yes …

KATHLEEN. Made Him a bachelor. Cor blimey: no wife for Him.

HARRY. No.

KATHLEEN. Saved somebody the trouble.

HARRY. Yes.

KATHLEEN. Does it all by telepathy.

HARRY. Yes.

KATHLEEN. Kids?

HARRY. What? … Oh … No.

KATHLEEN. Got married how old?

HARRY. Twenty er.

KATHLEEN. Man shouldn't marry till he's forty. Ridiculous. Don't know what they want till then. After that, too old to bother.

HARRY. Oh, yes.

KATHLEEN. Here …

(ALFRED *comes in carrying the chair. Sees them, nods; then goes back the way he's come.*)

Here! (*Calls after.*) That's where it's gone.

HARRY. Don't believe …

KATHLEEN. That's Alfred.

HARRY. Yes?

KATHLEEN. Wrestler.

HARRY. Yes.

KATHLEEN. Up here. (*Taps her head.*)

HARRY. Oh.

KATHLEEN. Where you going when you leave here?

HARRY. Well ... I ... er.

KATHLEEN. Lost your job?

HARRY. Well, I ...

KATHLEEN. Wife not have you?

HARRY. Well, I ...

KATHLEEN. Another man.

HARRY. Oh, now ...

KATHLEEN. Still ... Could be worse.

HARRY. Oh, yes.
    (*Pause*)

KATHLEEN. What's he want with that, then? Here ... you were
    slow to ask.

HARRY. Yes ...

KATHLEEN. You all right?

HARRY. Touch of the ... (*Wipes his eyes, nose.*)

KATHLEEN. Here, couple of old cry-babies you are. Bad as my
    friend.

HARRY. Yes ... Well ...

KATHLEEN. Shoot my brains out if I had a chance. Gawd! ...
    (*Feels her feet.*) Tried to kill myself with gas.

HARRY. Yes ... ?

KATHLEEN. Kiddies at my sister's. Head in oven. Knock on door,
    Milkman. Two weeks behind, he said. Broke everything.
    I did.

HARRY. Yes?

KATHLEEN. Nearly killed him. Would, too, if I could have got
    hold. Won't tap on our door, I can tell you. Not again.

HARRY. Goodness.

KATHLEEN. You all right?

HARRY. Yes ... I ... er.

KATHLEEN. Here. Hold my hand if you like.

HARRY. Oh, now.

KATHLEEN. Go on.

> (*Puts her hand on the table.*)
>
> Not much to look at.

HARRY. Oh, now. I wouldn't say that.

KATHLEEN. Go on.

HARRY. Well, I ... (*Takes her hand.*)

KATHLEEN. Our age: know what it's all about.

HARRY. Oh, well ... A long road, you know.

KATHLEEN. Can't get to old age fast enough for me. Sooner they put me under ...

HARRY. Oh, now ...

KATHLEEN. Different for a man.

HARRY. Well, I ...

KATHLEEN. I know. Have your troubles. Still. Woman's different.

HARRY. Oh, I ...

KATHLEEN. Wouldn't be a woman. Not again ... Here!

> (ALFRED *has entered. He goes past, upstage, carrying the chair. Glances at them. Goes off.*)
>
> Been here years, you know. Do the work of ten men if they set him to it.

HARRY. I say ... (*Looking off*)

KATHLEEN. Dunno where they've been ... (*Calls.*) Oi! ... Deaf as a post. Here, no need to let go ... Think you're shy.

HARRY. Oh, well ...

KATHLEEN. Never mind. Too old to be disappointed.

HARRY. Oh, now ...

> (JACK *and* MARJORIE *enter, the former carrying a wicker chair.*)

MARJORIE. Here you are, then. Been looking for you all over.

KATHLEEN. Been here, haven't we, all the time.

(HARRY *stands*.)

JACK. Sun still strong.

HARRY. Oh, yes.

MARJORIE. Here. Where's the other chair?

KATHLEEN. He's taken it over there.

MARJORIE. What's he doing?

KATHLEEN. Dunno. Here, sit on his knee if you want to!

MARJORIE. Catch me. Who do you think I am? (*Sits.*)

KATHLEEN. Well, no good you both standing.

JACK (*to* HARRY). No, no. After you, old man.

HARRY. No, no. After you ...

KATHLEEN. Be here all day, you ask me. Here, I'll stand ... Gawd ...

JACK. Oh, no ...

HARRY. Ridiculous.

MARJORIE. Take it in turns.

JACK. Right, I'll er.

HARRY. Do. Do. Go ahead.

JACK. Very decent. Very. (*Sits; sighs.*)

MARJORIE. Been carrying that around, looking for you, he has.

KATHLEEN. Been here, we have, all the time.

MARJORIE. What you been up to, then?

KATHLEEN. Nothing you might mind.

MARJORIE (*to* HARRY). Want to watch her. Men all the time.

KATHLEEN. One who knows.

MARJORIE. Seen it with my own eyes.

KATHLEEN. Lot more besides.

JACK. Think it might look up. Clearing ... (*Gazing up*)

HARRY. Oh. Very. (*Gazes up.*)

MARJORIE. Fallen in love, she has.

JACK. Damn nuisance about the chair, what?

HARRY. Oh. Very.

MARJORIE. Has to see the doctor about it, she has.

KATHLEEN. See the doctor about you, girl.

MARJORIE. Can't let no tradesman near the house. Five kids. Milkman, window-cleaner ...

KATHLEEN. Know your trouble, don't you?

MARJORIE. Nothing's bad as yours.

KATHLEEN. Can't go down the street without her trousers wetting.

JACK. Spot more sun, see those flowers out. Shouldn't wonder.

HARRY. Oh, yes.

JACK. By jove, Farrer, isn't it?

HARRY. Say he was a champion quarter-miler.

JACK. Shouldn't be surprised. Build of an athlete. Square shoulders.

HARRY. Deep chest.

JACK. Oh, yes.

KATHLEEN. You know what you should do with your mouth, girl.

MARJORIE. You know what you should do with something else.

KATHLEEN (to HARRY). Take a little stroll if you don't mind ... Gawd strewth ... (Gets up; HARRY hastens to help.)

MARJORIE. Mind she doesn't stroll you to the bushes.

KATHLEEN. Mind she doesn't splash.

MARJORIE. See the doctor about you, my girl!

KATHLEEN. See him all the time: your trouble. Not right in the head.

(KATHLEEN has taken HARRY's arm.
They go off.)

MARJORIE. Can't keep away from men.

JACK. Oh dear. (Gazing after)

MARJORIE. Gardens.

JACK. Oh.

MARJORIE. Parks especially.

JACK. I have heard of such er.

MARJORIE. Complaints. Used to send the police in threes. Can't
  trust two and one was never enough.

JACK. My word.

MARJORIE. Oh, yes.

JACK. Can never tell a leopard ...

MARJORIE. What? Should see her. Spots all over.

JACK. Oh dear.

MARJORIE. Never washes.

JACK. One of the advantages of a late lunch, of course, is that it
  leaves a shorter space to tea.

MARJORIE. What's your friend's name?

JACK. Harry ...

MARJORIE. What's he do, then?

JACK. Temporary er ... Thought a slight ...

MARJORIE. Get one with her all right. Have another.

JACK. Oh, yes ...

MARJORIE. Don't know what we're coming to.

JACK. Life ... mystery ... (*Gazes up.*)

  (MARJORIE *watches him. Then:*)

MARJORIE. What you put away for, then?

JACK. Oh ... what?

MARJORIE. In here.

JACK. Oh ... Little ...

MARJORIE. Girl?

JACK. Girl?

MARJORIE. Girls.

JACK. Girls?

MARJORIE. In the street.

JACK. Really? (*Looks around.*)

MARJORIE. Here ... What you in for?

JACK. A wholly voluntary basis, I assure you.

MARJORIE. Wife put you away?

JACK. Oh, no. No, no. Just a moment ... needed ... Thought I
  might ...

MARJORIE. Ever been in the padded whatsit?

JACK. Don't believe ... (*Looking around*)

MARJORIE. Here ... Don't tell my friend.

JACK. Oh, well ...

MARJORIE. Lie there for hours, you can.

JACK. Oh, now.

MARJORIE. Been here twice before.

JACK. Really ...

MARJORIE. Don't tell my friend.

JACK. Oh, no.

MARJORIE. Thinks it's my first.

JACK. Goodness ...

MARJORIE. One of the regulars. Wouldn't know what to do without me.

JACK. Oh, yes. Familiar faces.

MARJORIE. Come for three months; out again. Back again at Christmas.

JACK. Oh, yes.

MARJORIE. Can't stand Christmas.

JACK. No. Well. Season of festivities ... good cheer.

MARJORIE. Most people don't talk to you in here. You noticed?

JACK. Very rare. Well ... find someone to communicate.

MARJORIE. 'Course. Privileged.

JACK. Yes?

MARJORIE. Being in the reception wing.

JACK. Oh, yes.

MARJORIE. Good as cured.

JACK. Oh, yes.

MARJORIE. Soon be out.

JACK. Oh, goodness ... Hardly worth the trouble.

MARJORIE. No.

JACK. Home tomorrow!

MARJORIE. You been married long?

JACK. Oh, yes ... What?

64

MARJORIE. You in love?

JACK. What?

MARJORIE. Your wife.

JACK. Clouds ... This morning, my friend was remarking on the edges.

MARJORIE. Hardly worth the trouble.

JACK. Oh, yes.

MARJORIE. Going home.

JACK. Oh, well ... one has one's ... thought I might plant some seeds. Soil not too good, I notice ...

MARJORIE. Tell you something?

JACK. Oh, yes.

MARJORIE. Set up here for good.

JACK. Oh, yes.

MARJORIE. Here, you listening? What you in for?

JACK. Oh ...

MARJORIE. Here; you always crying.

JACK. Light ... eye ... (*Wipes his eye with his handkerchief.*)

MARJORIE. Tell you something.

JACK. Yes.

MARJORIE. Not leave here again.

JACK. Oh, no.

> (*They are silent.*
>
> ALFRED *comes on. He stands at the back, leaning on the chair.*)

MARJORIE. You going to sit on that or something?

ALFRED. What?

MARJORIE. Sit.

ALFRED. Dunno.

MARJORIE. Give it to somebody who can, you do.

ALFRED. What?

MARJORIE. Give it to somebody who can.

ALFRED. Yeh.

MARJORIE. You know my friend?

ALFRED. No.

E   65

MARJORIE. This is Alfred.

JACK. Oh ... Good ... day. (*Stands formally.*)

ALFRED. Where you get your cane?

JACK. Oh ... (*Looks down at it.*) Came with me.

ALFRED. I had a cane like that once.

JACK. Ah, yes.

ALFRED. Nicked it.

JACK. Oh, now.

MARJORIE. Had it when he came. Didn't you? Sit down.

JACK. Yes. (*Sits.*)

ALFRED. Wanna fight?

JACK. No ...

ALFRED. You?

MARJORIE. No, thanks.

ALFRED. Got sixpence?

JACK. No.

MARJORIE. Here. You seen my friend?

ALFRED. No.

MARJORIE. What you in for?

ALFRED. In what?

MARJORIE. Thinks he's at home, he does. Doesn't know his own strength, do you?

ALFRED. No.

MARJORIE. Took a bit of his brain, haven't they?

ALFRED. Yeh.

MARJORIE. Feel better?

ALFRED. Yeh.

MARJORIE. His mother's eighty-four.

ALFRED. Seventy.

MARJORIE. Thought you said she was eighty-four.

ALFRED. Seventy.

MARJORIE. Won't know his own name soon.

ALFRED. You wanna fight?

MARJORIE. Knock you down one hand behindmy back.

ALFRED. Garn.

MARJORIE. Half kill you, I will.

ALFRED. Go on.

MARJORIE. Wanna try? (*Stands.*)

(ALFRED *backs off a couple of steps.* MARJORIE *sits.*)

Take that chair off you, you don't look out.

JACK. Slight breeze. Takes the heat off the sun.

MARJORIE. Wanna jump on him if he bullies you.

JACK. Oh, yes.

MARJORIE (*to* ALFRED). What you looking at then?

ALFRED. Sky. (*Looks up.*)

MARJORIE. They'll lock you up if you don't look out. How old's your father?

ALFRED. Twenty-two.

MARJORIE. Older than him, are you?

ALFRED. Yeh.

MARJORIE. Older than his dad he is. Don't know where that leaves him.

JACK. Hasn't been born, I shouldn't wonder.

MARJORIE. No! (*Laughs.*) Hasn't been born, he shouldn't wonder. (*Pause*) Painted rude letters in the road.

ALFRED. Didn't.

MARJORIE. Did.

ALFRED. Didn't.

MARJORIE. Did. Right in the town centre. Took them three weeks to scrub it off.

ALFRED. Two.

MARJORIE. Three.

ALFRED. Two.

MARJORIE. Three. Apprentice painter and decorator. Didn't know what he was going to decorate. (*To* ALFRED) They'll apprentice you no more. (*To* JACK) Doesn't know his own strength, he doesn't.

JACK (*looking round*). Wonder where ...

MARJORIE. Send the police out for them, they will.

JACK. Clouds ... (*Looking up*)

MARJORIE. Seen it all, I have. Rape, intercourse. Physical pleasure.

JACK. I had a cousin once ...

MARJORIE. Here, you got a big family, haven't you?

JACK. Seven brothers and sisters. Spreads around, you know.

MARJORIE. Here, you was an only child last week.

JACK. A niece of mine—I say niece ... she was only ...

MARJORIE. What you do it for?

JACK. Oh, now ...

MARJORIE (*to* ALFRED). Wanna watch him. Trained as a doctor he has.

JACK. Wonder where ... (*Gazing round*)

MARJORIE (*to* ALFRED). What you paint in the road?

ALFRED. Nothing.

MARJORIE. Must have painted something. Can't paint nothing. Must have painted something or they couldn't have rubbed it off.

ALFRED. Paint you if you don't watch out.

MARJORIE. I'll knock your head off.

ALFRED. Won't.

MARJORIE. Will.

ALFRED. Won't.

MARJORIE. Will.

ALFRED. Won't.

MARJORIE. What you doing with that chair?

ALFRED. Nothing. (*Spins it beneath his hand.*)

MARJORIE. Faster than a rocket he is. Wanna watch him ... Where you going?

(JACK *has got up.*)

JACK. Thought I might ... Oh ...

(HARRY *and* KATHLEEN *have come on from the other side, the latter leaning on* HARRY's *arm.*)

68

KATHLEEN. Gawd ... they're coming off. I'll have nothing left ... Oh ...

(HARRY *helps her to the chair.*)

MARJORIE. Here, where you been?

KATHLEEN. There and back.

MARJORIE. Know where you been, my girl.

KATHLEEN. Don't.

HARRY. Canteen. We've ...

KATHLEEN. Don't tell her. Nose ten miles long she has. Trip over it one day she will. What's he doing?(*Indicating* ALFRED)

MARJORIE. Won't give up his chair, he won't.

HARRY. Still got three, what?

JACK. Yes ... what. Clouds ...

HARRY. Ah ... Rain.

JACK. Shouldn't wonder.

MARJORIE. Here. Put that chair down.

(ALFRED *still stands there.*

MARJORIE *stands.* ALFRED *releases the chair quickly.*)

(*To* JACK) You get it.

JACK. Er ... right.

(*Goes and gets the chair.* ALFRED *doesn't move.*)

MARJORIE. One each, then.

HARRY. Yes ...

MARJORIE. Well ... (*Indicates they sit.*)

KATHLEEN. Gawd ... (*Holds her feet.*)

MARJORIE. Had a job once.

KATHLEEN. Gawd.

MARJORIE. Packing tins of food.

KATHLEEN (*to* ALFRED). What you looking at?

ALFRED. Nothing.

MARJORIE. Pull your skirt down, girl.

KATHLEEN. Got nothing up mine ain't got up yours.

MARJORIE. Put them in cardboard boxes.

JACK. Really? I had a ...

MARJORIE. Done by machine now.

KATHLEEN. Nothing left for you to do, my girl. That's your trouble.

MARJORIE. 'Tis.

KATHLEEN. Cries everywhere, she does.

HARRY. Oh. One has one's ...

KATHLEEN. 'Specially at Christmas. Cries at Christmas. Boxing Day. Sometimes to New Year.

JACK. Oh, well, one ...

KATHLEEN (*indicating* ALFRED). What's he doing, then?

MARJORIE. Waiting to be born, he is.

KATHLEEN. What?

MARJORIE. Eight o'clock tomorrow morning. Better be there. (*Laughs. To* ALFRED) You better be there.

ALFRED. Yeh.

MARJORIE. Late for his own birthday, he is. (*To* ALFRED) Never catch up, you won't.

HARRY (*holding out hand; inspects it*). Thought I ... No.

JACK. Could be. (*Looks up.*)

HARRY. Lucky so far.

JACK. Oh, yes.

HARRY. Possibility ... (*Looking up*)

JACK. By jove ...

MARJORIE. One thing you can say about this place ...

KATHLEEN. Yes.

MARJORIE. 'S not like home.

KATHLEEN. Thank Gawd.

MARJORIE (*to* ALFRED). What you want?

ALFRED. Nothing.

KATHLEEN. Give you nothing if you come here ... What you staring at?

ALFRED. Nothing.

MARJORIE. Taken off a bit of his brain they have.

KATHLEEN (*to* ALFRED). Where they put it then?

MARJORIE. Thrown it in the dustbin.

KATHLEEN. Could have done with that. (*Laughs.*) Didn't cut a bit of something else off, did they?

MARJORIE. You know what your trouble is, my girl.

JACK. Time for tea, I shouldn't wonder. (*Stands.*)

HARRY. Yes. Well ... let me see. Very nearly.

JACK. Stretch the old legs ...

HARRY. Oh, yes.

MARJORIE. Not your legs need stretching, ask me.

JACK. Ah, well ... Trim. (*Bends arms; stretches.*)

MARJORIE. Fancies himself he does.

KATHLEEN. Don't blame him.

MARJORIE. Watch yourself, my girl.

KATHLEEN. No harm come from trying.

MARJORIE. Good job your feet like they are, ask me.

KATHLEEN. Have them off in the morning. Not stand this much longer.

MARJORIE. Slow her down; know what they're doing.

KATHLEEN. Know what she is?

JACK. Well, I ...

KATHLEEN. P.O.

JACK. P.O.

KATHLEEN. Persistent Offender.

MARJORIE. Ain't no such thing.

KATHLEEN. Is.

MARJORIE. Isn't.

KATHLEEN. Heard it in the office. Off Doctor ... what's his name.

MARJORIE. Never heard of that doctor, I haven't. Must be a new one must that. Doctor what's his name is a new one on me.

KATHLEEN. I know what I heard.

MARJORIE. Here. What's he crying about?

(HARRY *is drying his eyes.*)

KATHLEEN. Always crying one of these two.

MARJORIE. Call them the water babies, you ask me. (*To* ALFRED) You seen this?

(ALFRED *gazes woodenly towards them.*)

KATHLEEN. He's another.

MARJORIE. Don't know what'll become of us, girl.

KATHLEEN. Thought you was the one to cry.

MARJORIE. So d'I.

KATHLEEN. My dad was always crying.

MARJORIE. Yeh?

KATHLEEN. Drank too much. Came out of his eyes.

MARJORIE. Ooh! (*Laughs, covering her mouth.*)

KATHLEEN. Here, what's the matter with you, Harry?

HARRY. Oh, just a er.

JACK. Could have sworn ... (*holds out hand; looks up.*)

KATHLEEN. 'S not rain. 'S him. Splashing it all over, he is.

JACK. There, now ...

MARJORIE. Here. Look at him: thinks it's raining.

KATHLEEN (*to* JACK). Here. Your friend ...

(JACK *breathes deeply: fresh-air exercises.*)

JACK. Freshening.

MARJORIE. I don't know. What they come out for?

KATHLEEN. Crying all over, they are.

MARJORIE (*to* JACK). You going to help your friend, then, are you?

JACK. Oh. Comes and goes ...

KATHLEEN (*to* HARRY). Wanna hold my hand?

(HARRY *doesn't answer.*)

MARJORIE. Not seen so many tears. Haven't.

KATHLEEN. Not since Christmas.

MARJORIE. Not since Christmas, girl.

KATHLEEN. Ooooh!

MARJORIE (*to* JACK). You all right?

(JACK *doesn't answer. Stands stiffly turned away, looking off.*)

Think you and I better be on our way, girl.

KATHLEEN. Think we had.

MARJORIE. Try and make something. What you get for it?

KATHLEEN. Get nothing if you don't try, girl.

MARJORIE. No.

KATHLEEN. Get nothing if you do, either.

MARJORIE. Ooooh! (*Laughs, covering her mouth; stands.*) Don't slow you down, do they? (*Indicates shoes.*)

KATHLEEN. Get my laces back or else, girl ... Oh! (*Winces, standing. To* ALFRED) What you staring at?

ALFRED. Nothing.

KATHLEEN. Be dead this time tomorrow.

MARJORIE. No complaints then, my girl.

KATHLEEN. Not too soon for me.

MARJORIE. Going to say goodbye to your boy-friend?

KATHLEEN. Dunno that he wants to know ...

MARJORIE. Give you a hand, girl?

KATHLEEN. Can't move without.

MARJORIE. There ... on our way.

KATHLEEN. Gawd.

MARJORIE. Not stop here again.

KATHLEEN. Better get out of here, girl ... Gawd! Go mad here you don't watch out.

> (*Groaning,* KATHLEEN *is led off by* MARJORIE.
> *Pause.*
> ALFRED *comes up. Holds table, waits, then lifts it. Raises it above his head. Turns. Walks off.*)

JACK. By jove.

> (HARRY *stirs.*)

Freshening ... Surprised if it doesn't blow over by tomorrow.

HARRY. Oh, yes ...

JACK. Saw Harrison yesterday.

HARRY. Yes?

JACK. Congestion.

HARRY. Soot.

JACK. Really?

HARRY. Oh, yes. (*Dries his eyes.*)

JACK. Shouldn't wonder if wind veers. North-west.

HARRY. East.

JACK. Really? Higher ground, of course, one notices.

HARRY. Found the er. (*Gestures after* MARJORIE *and* KATHLEEN.)

JACK. Oh, yes.

HARRY. Extraordinary.

JACK. 'Straordinary.

HARRY. Get used to it after a while.

JACK. Oh, yes ... I have a sister-in-law, for example, who wears dark glasses.

HARRY. Really?

JACK. Each evening before she goes to bed.

HARRY. Really.

JACK. Following morning: takes them off.

HARRY. Extraordinary.

JACK. Sunshine—never wears them.

HARRY. Well ... I ... (*Finally wipes his eyes and puts his handkerchief away.*) Extraordinary.

JACK. The older one grows, of course ... the more one takes into account other people's foibles.

HARRY. Oh, yes.

JACK. If a person can't be what they are, what's the purpose of being anything at all?

HARRY. Oh, absolutely.

(ALFRED *has returned. He picks up one of the metalwork chairs; turns it one way then another, gazes at Jack and Harry, then slowly carries it off.*)

JACK. I suppose in the army, of course, one becomes quite used to foibles.

HARRY. Oh, yes.

JACK. Navy, too, I shouldn't wonder.

HARRY. Oh, yes.

74

JACK. A relative of mine rose to lieutenant-commander in a seagoing corvette.

HARRY. My word.

JACK. In the blood.

HARRY. Bound to be.

JACK. Oh, yes. Without the sea: well, hate to think.

HARRY. Oh, yes.

JACK. At no point is one more than seventy-five miles from the sea.

HARRY. Really.

JACK. That is the nature of this little island.

HARRY. Extraordinary when you think.

JACK. When you think what came from it.

HARRY. Oh, yes.

JACK. Radar.

HARRY. Oh, yes.

JACK. Jet propulsion.

HARRY. My word.

JACK. Television.

HARRY. Oh ...

JACK. Steam-engine.

HARRY. Goodness.

JACK. Empire the like of which no one has ever seen.

HARRY. No. My word.

JACK. Light of the world.

HARRY. Oh, yes.

JACK. Penicillin.

HARRY. Penicillin.

JACK. Darwin.

HARRY. Darwin.

JACK. Newton.

HARRY. Newton.

JACK. Milton.

HARRY. My word.

JACK. Sir Walter Raleigh.

HARRY. Goodness. Sir ...

JACK. Lost his head.

HARRY. Oh, yes.

JACK. This little island.

HARRY. Shan't see its like.

JACK. Oh, no.

HARRY. The sun has set.

JACK. Couple of hours ...

HARRY. What?

JACK. One of the strange things, of course, about this place.

HARRY. Oh, yes.

JACK. Is its size.

HARRY. Yes.

JACK. Never meet the same people two days running.

HARRY. No.

JACK. Can't find room, of course.

HARRY. No.

JACK. See them at the gates.

HARRY. Oh, my word.

JACK. Of an evening, looking in. Unfortunately the money isn't there.

HARRY. No.

JACK. Exchequer. Diverting wealth to the proper ...

HARRY. Oh, yes.

JACK. Witness: one metalwork table, two metalwork chairs; two thousand people.

HARRY. My word, yes.

JACK. While overhead ...

HARRY. Oh, yes ...

(*They both gaze up.*

ALFRED *comes in; he picks up the remaining white chair.*)

ALFRED. You finished?

JACK. What ... ?

ALFRED. Take them back. (*Indicates their two wicker chairs.*)

HARRY. Oh, yes ...

ALFRED. Don't take them back: get into trouble.

JACK. Oh, my word.

> (ALFRED, *watching them, lifts the metal chair with one hand, holding its leg; demonstrates his strength.*
> *They watch in silence.*
> ALFRED *lifts the chair above his head; then, still watching them, turns and goes.*)

Shadows.

HARRY. Yes.

JACK. Another day.

HARRY. Ah, yes.

JACK. Brother-in-law I had was an artist.

HARRY. Really?

JACK. Would have appreciated those flowers. Light fading ... Clouds.

HARRY. Wonderful thing.

JACK. Oh, yes.

HARRY. Would have liked to have been an artist myself. Musician.

JACK. Really?

HARRY. Flute.

JACK. Beautiful instrument.

HARRY. Oh, yes.

> (*They gaze at the view.*)

HARRY. Shadows.

JACK. Choose any card ... (*Holds pack out from his pocket.*)

HARRY. Any?

JACK. Any one ...

HARRY (*takes one*). Yes ... !

JACK. Eight of Diamonds.

HARRY. My word!

JACK. Right?

HARRY. Absolutely.

JACK. Intended to show the ladies.

HARRY. Another day.

JACK. Oh, yes.

(JACK *re-shuffles cards; holds them out.*)

HARRY. Again?

JACK. Any one.

HARRY. Er ...

JACK. Three of Spades.

HARRY. Two of Hearts.

JACK. What? (*Inspects the cards briefly; puts them away.*)

HARRY. Amazing thing, of course, is the er.

JACK. Oh, yes.

HARRY. Still prevails.

JACK. Oh, my goodness.

HARRY. Hendricks I find is a ...

JACK. Oh, yes.

HARRY. Moustache ... Eye-brows.

JACK. Divorced.

HARRY. Oh, yes.

JACK. Moral fibre. Set to a task, never complete it. Find some way to back out.

HARRY. Oh, yes.

JACK. The sea is an extraordinary ...

HARRY. Oh, yes.

JACK. Cousin of mine ...

HARRY. See the church.

(*They gaze off.*)

JACK. Shouldn't wonder He's disappointed. (*Looks up.*)

HARRY. Oh, yes.

JACK. Heart-break.

HARRY. Oh, yes.

JACK. Same mistake ... Won't make it twice.

HARRY. Oh, no.

JACK. Once over. Never again.

    (ALFRED *has come on.*)

ALFRED. You finished?

JACK. Well, I ... er ...

ALFRED. Take 'em back.

JACK. Oh, well. That's very ...

    (ALFRED *grasps the two wicker chairs. Glances at* JACK *and* HARRY; *picks up both the chairs.*

    Glances at JACK *and* HARRY *again, holding the chairs. Takes them off.*)

  What I ... er ... yes.

    (HARRY *has begun to weep.*

    JACK *gazes off.*

    A moment later JACK *also wipes his eyes.*

    After a while the light slowly fades.)

CURTAIN